THE GREAT CONCIERGE

FULL HOSPITALITY GUIDE AND CUSTOMER CARE SECRETS

VALERIO A. SIMULA

ACKNOWLEDGMENTS

 The information contained in this book was gathered from conversations, interviews and the first-hand experiences of my father and me, while working in the hospitality industry for many years.

 It will never be enough to thank my father Luciano for making me the person I am now, because of him I have learned invaluable secrets and tips that have developed my career.

 Unfortunately he has died too early to see how I have excelled in the hospitality industry, following his example. It is my sincere hope that he is proud of me as he looks down from the heavens.

 I'm indebted to my wife, Liudmila, for her love and patience as the demands of my job interpose on our private life.

 A special thanks to my editor for her extraordinary help in editing this book.

I owe a debt of gratitude to all of my colleagues both past and present who have influenced and impacted my life in some way; helping me to grow in my career.

And a thank you to all my readers. Thank you so much!

 All the stories and the names are invented. The purpose of these stories is to help readers to better understand and to give examples of the situations that may have occurred. The privacy of our guests is paramount, therefore all events are coincidental.

Table of Contents

Introduction

Having a father with a passion for the hospitality industry is perhaps the major reason that I too have fallen in love with it. In my life I have known many good concierges but very few great ones like my father. He was exceptional and taught me the ins and outs of this profession.

In this book you will get the opportunity to learn many of the things that he taught me. I will share with you detailed information from my own experiences and knowledge as a qualified concierge, about what you need to know and do to become a great concierge, and how to be successful in this career.

My father always wanted me to follow in his foot-steps and choose a similar profession as his by becoming a concierge. At the early age of eleven, I was introduced to the amazing world of hospitality. You see, my father was born in the wonderful island of Sardinia, Italy's largest island with beautiful beaches that lured visitors from all over the world to vacation at the hotels in Sardinia. It was in these hotels that my father worked for his entire life and learned to be a master in his field.

As a young and energetic man he started working during the summer as a waiter in the seasonal hotel restaurants.

However, after getting married he and his wife decided to leave the island to live in the business and fashion city of Milan.

It was an exciting time for him and little did he know that his move would facilitate the growth of his long career in the hotel industry.

One day, he eagerly accepted his friend's offer to work in a five-star hotel in the city center as a receptionist . It is there that he worked for 10 years before deciding to move to a smaller hotel in Milan where he started as concierge near the Milan City Fair.

"I never imagined that this job could be so nice! I loved it from the very first day and I will never change it for anything else." Those words from my father were etched in my memory from the time I was eleven years - old. In response I asked him: "What's so different about it from your previous job as a receptionist?" With great excitement in his voice he replied,"There are many differences, not only from my previous job; this is true passion! If you could only understand what I mean, you would love it just like I do now."

At that time I could not understand what he was saying, but his excitement created a curiosity within me. So I asked him to show me what his job was about.

He agreed and during the night shift when the manager was absent he took me with him. I never will forget that particular occasion, when my father as he promised took me to work. It was during the summer holidays so I could sleep late the day after. He bought me an elegant suit and taught me how to make the tie knot in front of the mirror. Wow! I looked like a little man and I was so excited.

The first night that I went with him, he told me to wait in the lobby while he changed his clothes. After a few minutes he introduced me to two of his colleagues who were about to finish the shift and to another colleague who was starting the night shift as well. For the first five minutes I was a bit shy but then after they offered me candies and a fruit juice and smiled with me I felt very comfortable. I was also nicknamed Mr.Simula, Jr.

It was a really fantastic experience. People from different countries and nationalities speaking several languages visited that hotel. I felt so proud of my father that night and from behind the desk I watched how he and his workmate interacted with their clients. They handled them politely, calmly and with such kindness as they greeted each other like longtime friends simply doing a favor. My father from time to time would instruct the bellboy to take items to the guests in their rooms. He was very detailed and made certain that the bellboy knew how to do it. There was no doubt that my father really loved his job, even when speaking on the phone he wore an effervescent smile.

To my surprise, for the first time I realized that my father could speak Deutsch, English, French, Japanese and Chinese. "How did you learn all those languages?" I asked him. That night he looked at me and said, "Son, I didn't learn them at school, and I don't speak all the languages fluently, but what is most important is that you can understand your guests and they can understand you."

Truth is though, that one of the highlights of going to work with my dad was getting the tips. When the guest gave them to my father, he would pass them onto me. I had big plans for them so I hoped that all the guest would be kind. I would have plenty of money to spend on video games in the bar near my home.

I got my first tour of a hotel that night when my dad asked the bellboy to show me around. He took me to the restaurant, the bar, the gym and the spa. But even though I was happy about those things, it was really the jacuzzi that tickled my fancy. I was simply fascinated by it - it was like a dream. After the tour, I got the opportunity to accompany some Italian guests to their room as Italian was the only language that I could speak. Of course my father gave detailed instructions as he usually did. "Only call the elevator" he said calmly "escort the guest to their room and once you are there, turn on the lights and show them where to find the safety deposit box."

As I reflect on those experiences I am elated, not because I got even more tips to play video games but because my father had such confidence in me.

I was very happy and lucky that he gave me the opportunity to work with him during the summer every time he was on duty at night shift .

It was there that I learned more about this fantastic job and I started to understand his passion and love for the hotel industry.
Gradually, I understood how to use the computer and I could take request in other languages.
By the end of the summer holidays, I was able to assist some Italian guest with easy things like booking tours and restaurant reservations - with my father's help of course.

"There are two persons who earn lots of money at the hotel, the first is the concierge and the second is the hotel manager."

Those words were often said to me by my father as if he meant to give me yet another reason to choose a career in the industry. In reality though, that was true up to 10 years ago, now guests leave tips only if you have solved a difficult problem and sometimes even then they don't.

Nevertheless, I think that this advice is still valid along with the fact that my father also repeated to me several times that, "the passion should be the only reason that you are attracted to this job, if you want to be successful".

.My father made a big difference in my choice of career. Even to this day I still communicate with many people who he introduced me to when I was a young boy. At such a young age, I recognized that I too was becoming intrigued by this type of work. When my father took our family out for dinner, I can remember every restaurant owner coming at our table upon arrival and after dinner to thank him. We were treated like VIP and sometimes got gifts, like a good bottle of wine.

I followed my father's advice and joined the Hotel school "Carlo Porta" in Milan, a professional institute providing studies in hotel hospitality, hotel management and hotel reception.
This school is reputed to be the best in the city with lots of practical exercises and work simulations and teaches English, French and Deutsch. There is a strict dress code and students must wear suits.

I was extremely fortunate to be a part of the internship program organized by the school, allowing us to work for a month in a five- star hotel in Milan. My stints were at Principe di Savoia, Hotel Pierre and Hotel Duomo and in the last year, we had the coveted experience of managing an entire hotel for two months in the small city of Aprica in the Orobie Alps; working 8 hours per day including night shift.

My professor or "hotel secretary" Mr. Ferruccio Zanchi is a man of infinite experience who I would never forget.

He continued from where my father left off in increasing my passion for working at the hotel. One day he told me in private: "You will be ready to open and manage your own hotel after this college, but if you want be successful let the job guide you to the right position, don't force your choice or you will never be fulfilled in your work."Those words were profound and true because many people seek after professions just to make a lot of money and perhaps have freedom, yet they are not happy or successful.

The last day of our journey through school was very emotional, everyone was sad to leave the team that our professor had formed We were no longer just classmates, but a team consumed by a love for the hospitality industry and earnest to go out, face the world and be the best in our field.

I am now 37 years old and I am happy to say that I am chef concierge at Double Tree by Hilton Milan,where I started working immediately after it was built 8 years ago.

I am also a member of the prestigious company of the golden keys "Les clef d'Or" an international organization created in 1929 by concierges in France. Thanks to their strict rules and statutes, members are guaranteed up to two pins on the uniform they wear(the two crossed keys of gold symbol that dates back to the keeper of the keys in the medieval period, which are now created in partnership with Swiss jeweler Bucherer).

Today, I credit my father for my success as a concierge. There was no better example, no greater concierge whom I could mentor than my dad. I consider it a privilege to have had someone to give me helpful advice and chart the course for such a wonderful career. He inspired me and I caught his passion. My father taught me how to excel as a concierge and how to make the impossible become possible.

That is why I decided to write this book, so that I too can be an inspiration to those persons who have an interest in a career in the hospitality industry. It is my desire to pass on all that I have learned from my father, my professor and my own experiences to motivate you and push you into your destiny. In addition, I hope to open up your mind to how working in this field could benefit your personal development, improve your quality of life and generally speaking, provide opportunities and challenges that you never dreamed of.

Union International Les Clefs d'Or U.I.C.H.

Union International Les Clefs d'Or U.I.C.H is a worldwide network of professional concierges of hotels, grouped into national sections.

The motto of the association is "In service through friendship."

This not only applies to how the concierges approach their guest but also how they respect, communicate and work with each other throughout the hotel industry.

In order to register you must have experience working at a four or five star hotel for at least 5 years. At least two of those years should be in a concierge position. Additionally, you must be sponsored by two active members of the association council.

After two years of being an aspiring member you become an active member and finally you can wear the golden keys on the jacket lapel of the uniform. This is considered a great achievement but it is not completed unless you have done a written and oral exam, which evaluates your knowledge about the association and information about your city and country.

However, if you are not successful then, there is the opportunity to try again the following year.

The local association in Milan organizes several meetings every month. They are well-attended and you can engage with very nice people of like passion and establish beautiful friendships.

Business contact information is exchanged and we get to learn new things from senior members with a wealth of information about the industry, having worked in it all their lives just as my father did.

Monthly meetings of the council are open to all members. It is at these meetings that new initiatives are discussed and there is also a look at the association's financial position. The association also publishes its own monthly magazine, which is distributed for free in all hotels and provides the best maps and shopping maps of the city.

Very often after these meetings we visit different restaurants for dinner, where we receive warm greetings from the owners who are really very happy to be known by so many concierges. Apart from socializing, it also is a good networking opportunity for making new contacts, and staying up to date about the city and other important aspects of the industry.

I am particularly interested in and have participated in the many educational events in the local outlets, museums and excursions outside the city, which are organized for free by the association.

These trips have also taken us to Lugano Switzerland to visit the Swiss luxury watch maker Bucherer who create the crossed golden keys pin symbol of the association. It was an experience of a lifetime and all the members were offered a Lugano lake tour and then a delightful dinner overlooking the lake.

The national council hold their meetings annually and the world council every four years. My favorite event is the awards gala dinner for members. It is a spectacular affair with dinner, dance shows, singers and music.

The Milan Council headed by the President Sami Zeiter in collaboration with the vice President Bernie Gallotta, is doing a really good job and there is rapid growth in membership.

Additionally, they are introducing free training courses and have plans to double the free social activity for members in the next years, I'm honored to be part of it.

The power of the association is that we are all connected and ready to give support to other colleagues. It doesn't matter if they are in the other side of the planet. If it is your ambition to excel as a concierge in the hotel industry, then aspiring to become a member of the Union Internationale Les Clefs d'Or U.I.C.H is a good place to begin.

Chapter One

Being a Concierge

So you have decided that the hotel industry is where you want to be in terms of your career goals, more specifically you want to be a concierge. Or perhaps you are just a bit curious like I was in the beginning. Whichever is the case, in this chapter you will learn all about what a concierge is and does and how to excel in the profession.

For starters let's get some further insight into what a concierge is.

Concierge comes from the word in French "comte des cierges" meaning in English "keeper of the candles," this was the person who followed the guests of the medieval castles. Over the years the word has been aptly ascribed to persons working in the hotels, who "follow" their guests to ensure that they have an enjoyable experience during their stay. Concierges are hospitality ambassadors, who represent not only the hotel where they are working, but the entire association.

However, before you can become a great concierge, you must first be able to clearly identify and understand who the most important people are in your job and why.

Who are these people without whom your job would be unnecessary and non-existent? They are your customers, your guests and if you aspire to greatness they must become an important part of your world.

You need to ask yourself who are those guests, why do they spend thousands of dollars to stay in a luxury hotel and what are they looking for?

The reply to those questions is simple, they are looking for an experience, for a memory, they want something from you, you are the person who connects them to your services and amenities.

You must be able to create these experiences that they are looking for. To achieve this result, it is important that you establish high standards. Without the application of such standards by you and all the staff, you cannot guarantee your guests the experience that they are looking for.

Along with the responsibilities of maintaining high hospitality standards you must also be passionate about your job.
Having to work in the forefront, where they represent the hotel and are always in communication with the guests, they can either enhance or spoil a visitors vacation.
Certainly, in this industry, the customer is "king." Therefore a good concierge's aim is to always ascertain what the needs are of the guests and make every effort to meet them.

My father once asked me: "Can you tell me what is the difference between a specialist, a cultured person and a concierge?' I thought about it but as hard as I tried, I could not find the answer.

It was simple, he said, "the specialist is a person who knows everything in his field, the cultured person is a person who knows a bit in many fields, while the concierge knows everything about everything."

I can't imagine that there is any job that is more challenging but is at the same time totally rewarding. It is possible that you can wake up, go to work and be presented with numerous requests, some easy, some challenging and others virtually impossible to meet; it can be very demanding.
You have to be always ready for anything.

It's nice to help other people. It makes you feel really good when someone comes back to thank you by just holding your hand or to give you a small reward.
A job well done and a satisfied guest can make you forget the stress accumulated during the day. Making every guest feel important must be the goal of our business, we do not have to judge them when they ask for a service, because when we give a service we should not judge those who request it, our work does not allow that.
All guests should be treated like celebrities.

There are some key elements involved in making your guests happy that every concierge should know. Remember, people don't come on vacation just to stay in the hotel.

They want to see the country, explore the city, meet the people and experience the food and culture of the place. So how do you as a concierge make that happen? By networking - one of the most important factors of having a successful business and sales venture.

Create a close network of contacts who have great ideas and a variety of activities to offer that would give your clients a unique experience and make their stay more pleasant and enjoyable.

Secondly, having good communication skills and maintaining a good reputation will prove to be assets. You will definitely need them to be efficient and effective. As a concierge you will be in contact with several people on a daily basis, including customers, suppliers and your colleagues from all the other hotels. Therefore, being able to interact with these individuals is absolutely vital.

My father always said, "Remain humble with your customers, you're nobody without them! The greater the guests' demands the more you and your reputation will grow." If you really want to excel as a concierge and make your guests happy as a result, you cannot ignore the fact that you must guard your character.

Keeping a good reputation is very important for the concierge; being polite, generous and honest are all a part of it. It takes a long time to build a good reputation, but just a few minutes to tear it down. Be careful not to let that happen to you.

Certainly it is very important what category of hotel you are working at. It really does matter! If you are working at a luxury hotel where there are several VIP guests and many rooms it will facilitate the growth of your reputation.

My father told me once that when he was working in a four-star hotel which was more decentralized and with less rooms, that he had difficulty securing a last minute reservation at any of the best restaurants in the city. This was so because their policy was that reservations had to be made one week in advance.

Additionally, concierges working at the five-start luxury hotels with more rooms were always given preference. Of course the guests staying in these hotels were from the higher echelons of society, namely the rich and famous.

So what does a concierge in a lower rated hotel do? How can this challenge be overcome? Take my father's advice - find a way to befriend the owners of the restaurants in the city. Take the time out to visit their establishments and be visible to them.

That way you are no longer just the concierge on the phone but someone who they have developed a relationship with; they now know you. My father used this method successfully and discovered that some of the owners actually came from his hometown Sardinia Island and they spoke in dialect by phone; that's how his reservations were given priority over the others.

Don't be misled by the thought that because you may have the best qualifications on paper that will suffice. The reality is that the hospitality industry is not only looking for people with degrees.

Character, passion and a love for this field are definitely the most important qualities that they seek. They want people who are honest and motivated and have strong leadership abilities.

Of course, it is always advised that you do pursue your degree, to assist with your advancement. To this end schools for concierges have been opened in recent years in many countries all over the world.

Alternatively, you can take the initiative and ensure that you have excellent knowledge of the city firsthand and be fluent in the main foreign languages. It is very useful to try different experiences outside of your own country, but this is just a start.

Keep up to date and of course become an active member of your local Golden Keys association and exchange information with colleagues of the other hotels.

Having these contacts are for the mutual benefit of everyone concerned. We need them and they need us because the hotel concierge can expand their businesses.

Many establishments in the city offering different categories of services are indebted to the concierges because without their recommendations, they probably would not have the amount of guests that they do visiting their operations.

On several occasions these providers have called me to say thanks for referring guests who spent a lot of money in their business. Many of them indicated that these persons purchased thousands of dollars for famous Italian clothing, jewelry and watches.

The biggest purchase to date was when a guest bought $250,000 dollars worth in furniture and décor from a home furnishing shop for his home in Russia. Additionally, guest also spend thousands of dollars for bottles of champagne in the night clubs and to eat in the best Italian restaurants.

My father always said to me, "When you offer your service or your assistance to guests, let them feel like if they are paying less for it than the real value. If they rent a private jet service for $50,000 dollars let them feel like if the value for the service it's $300,000. You need to acclaim your product when you are selling to them and highlight the advantages and the high value of your services."

When some guests ask me for expensive services, I always like to give them two or more options with a different budget. I explain to them why there is a price difference and all the additional factors that make it more expensive.
Most of the time they choose the more expensive option because they are focused more on the best services and memories not the price.

Grooming and hygiene

Have you ever been to a business, where an employee was not well-groomed?
What was your first impression of that person?
Secondly, what was your impression of the business?
How you look and smell says a lot about you, and personal hygiene is part of the package.

It is important that you present yourself well and maintain the highest standards. You do not only represent yourself but also the hotel; your appearance must be impeccable!

To help you in the area of personal grooming and hygiene here are some rules to follow that I've learned during my studies and from personal experience:

Uniform
Always wear clean well-pressed uniforms.
Always wear the crossed golden keys on each lapel of your jacket.

Shoes
Ensure that your shoes are clean and polished before going on duty.

Females must wear appropriate stockings with black court shoes where the heels do not exceed two inches.

Males must wear black socks and shoes.

Hygiene

Take a bath daily.
Brush your hair before going on duty.
Brush your teeth daily.
Ensure that your nails are well-trimmed, and female staff should only wear clear or pale nail polish.

Hair
Female hair with length beyond the shoulders must be neatly tied/ bundled.
Men must have short well-combed hair.
Do not use unnatural hair-colors e.g. green, blue, unnatural blond etc.

Accessories
Only one ring and watch is permitted; small earrings for female staff.
Earrings, beards and moustaches are forbidden for male staff (in some hotels beards and moustaches are allowed only if well-groomed).
Lipstick of a suitable color must be worn at all times by females.
Only light and natural looking make-up is allowed.

Attitude

Be aware of your posture, never lean on the wall or with our back turned to the guests.

Never speak with your colleagues about other guest, while in the presence of another guest.

Never say no or I can not

"If someone ask you for an orange elephant, tell him maybe you can find a pink one," my father once said to me. Never start your sentence by saying "I can't" or "no." There's always an alternative - offer it! If you are really unable to fulfill the request always use the opportunity to offer an equal or better option.

The only things you should say "I can't" or "no" to are immoral or illegal requests or to have free tickets for "La Prima" at the Teather "La Scala" in Milan. You need to inform the guest that it's very unlikely that you can satisfy the latter request because it would be extremely hard to do.

Don't misunderstand what I am saying. Even though you should never say "no" initially, it is also totally wrong to say "yes," if you know that you can't do something. You will damage the relationship you have with the guest and trust will be lost. It is absolutely important that if you say yes that it must be yes, you need to be honest and sincere.

Don't take too much time to reply to them when they need your service. Be clear about your role and know what you can and cannot do. If they make a request you consider strange, one that you have never heard before, don't panic.
Even if you are nervous on the inside never let it show.

Of course they will not trust your suggestions if they see that you are not prepared. Simply reply by saying something like: "That's a good request let me check and find out." Right away you show them that you are interested, you have the skills to do what is required and you are actively pursuing their request.

That kind of response will build their trust in you. I use it sometimes when I don't know or I don't remember something. It's the best reply to give instead of making the guest feel that you are not informed well enough to help them.

How Become not a Good but a Great Concierge

When I was young, I went with my family to Greece for the summer holidays and we rented a room in a wonderful hotel near the beach.

From the moment we arrived we were treated with hospitality and care. It's not that I had a fantastic luxury room - quite the contrary, it was not that special. I can even remember my bed being in a strange position because the room wasn't large enough to put it in the right place. But, the service was excellent!

Particularly they took care of all of our needs during our stay. We found a welcome letter in the room written in Italian, in the minibar there was complimentary water and a bottle of wine from their white wine collection.

Clean beach towels every morning, a welcome drink at the bar and warm smiling faces kept their guests happy and satisfied. For the two weeks that we spent there, I never saw a guest mad with them. Care is indeed the core of every service.

The employees at that hotel cared enough to create a relationship with us, and we felt as though we were a part of one big family. So much so that I thought the employees of the hotel were all brothers and sisters or cousins, but I asked and they weren't.

Before you start to work in the hospitality industry be sure that you like the job. To succeed in this field you must like working with the public. I remember once that I visited a famous restaurant with a chain of outlets well known for great pizza.

To my surprise when I entered, no one came to help me find a seat; I did so on my own and found a table that was still not cleared. After a few minutes a waitress came to my table, cleaned it, left the menu and said,"What would you like to drink?" She never said "hello" or "welcome to this restaurant." To make matters worse, there was no smile, only a quick question without eye contact as she was looking at other tables while asking.

Anyway, I ordered one beer and without looking at the menu my favorite pizza, because I did not feel comfortable. The pizza was excellent, but the service was horrific because I was treated like just another part on an assembly line.

I don't know if it was only a bad day at the restaurant, because I've never been back.
That's exactly what your guest will do, if they are made to feel like they are intruding on your time or that they are just another set of visitors. They will leave and never return.

So before you accept an offer to work in the field of hospitality, interacting with people must be something you enjoy. Then once you are at work, you must leave your problems at home. Before you start your shift you need to stamp a smile on your face every day.

One of the main reasons why some businesses in the hospitality industry experience poor service delivery is because too many people who work for them neither enjoy their job nor have a passion for it. It is important therefore that managers find those employees, listen to them and let them know that there is a lot of potential for growth in their career and also their personal development.

However, if the individual continues to show little interest in improving and being a part of the team, it is best to release them and let them pursue another field.

Otherwise these employees can damage the image of the best of hotels as they are unable to maintain a high level of service and can create conflict if they are not team players.

All employees must work hard to reach the same goals.

"Knowledge is power. You can't begin a career, for that matter even a relationship, unless you know everything there is to know about it." Randeep Hooda

A great concierge should know everything possible about the hotel at which he is employed.

To re-emphasize the point, he must also remain fully aware of the services and attractions offered by the city in which he pursues his profession, and above all is a person who likes this job.

No matter what kind of education you pursued before embarking on a career as a concierge, having first-hand knowledge about your hotel is vital.
Of course having attended a university in the field of tourism or of hospitality, even though not indispensable is also important.

Throughout my career, I have had the privilege of meeting some concierges who graduated with degrees in art or architecture, then to realize that they wanted to work in a job where they were in contact with people and not just spend their life behind a desk in an office.

The job of the concierge is not at all easy as some might believe, it requires patience and hard work inside and outside the hotel.

Concierges in their free time should always keep informed about events that are in the cities and always be updated in order to exceed service expectations.
Do not depend solely on the internet! Keep yourself abreast of all the happenings around you.
As a concierge you should know and experience firsthand all about the city's events; their dates, times, why they are held and such like.

This knowledge will impress your clients but it will also give them a sense of security and interest. It gives your clients a great deal of satisfaction when they can make informed choices about where they will spend their time and money to be entertained.

Serving your clients at the highest standard means moving out of your hotel and hitting the streets on foot. Explore the city for yourself. Discover new and exciting attractions.
Get to know the ins and outs about the landmarks, attractions, restaurants and all the activities that will enhance the visitor's overall experience. Memorize the services and then extend your knowledge to wider areas.

From my experience business owners, event organizers and people in general are very welcoming when you let them know your good intentions and inquire about their services.

You want to see if what they have is compatible with the needs of your clients. Of course because they know the importance of a concierge, they will be happy to establish a mutually satisfying relationship. You make your guest happy and it helps their business. Everyone is a winner!

How to get started

You need to start by knowing all the features of your hotel, take notes and ask questions.

Find out from your members in various departments what is important to the guests from their end.

For a first-hand experience of the city visit:

Shopping resources - Malls, boutiques etc.

Entertainment resources- Movies, live stages, music concerts, dance clubs etc.

Sport resources -Tennis courts, golf courses, football matches etc.

Culture resources - Museums, art galleries etc.

Kid-friendly resources- Amusement parks, aquariums, zoos etc.

Dining resources- Restaurants etc.

Fun in the sun or winter resources - local beaches, bicycle rental, ski etc.

The great concierge should be very organized, in order to manage hundreds of contacts from different sectors and find them quickly.
Keep your e-mail very tidy. Have the list of the restaurants and organizations in a binder with all the cards and menus always updated.

It is better to divide them by area if you work in a big city. The address book contact numbers must be divided by categories and areas and in alphabetical order. In other words be as meticulous as a stamp collector and always keep the desk clean.

After many years I still write down every request. I write down the guests names, room numbers, the request time and what the guest asked for in detail. Additionally, I have a database of all guests requests to which I add their feedback. Taking notes helps you to avoid mistakes and do a better job.

When you visit the restaurants ask as many questions as possible and try their services. Take a look at the menus. Ask them if they can send you a copy of the menu by email. Leave your business card and write down everything that you notice from the point of view of a guest.

Hire a guide and visit all the city museums.

Hire a personal shopper to show you the most important shops in your city.

When you become a hotel expert you will find that your interactions with guests are easier and more satisfying. They will see your professional "hospitality."

Chapter two

Anticipate your guests' needs

The secret to understanding what a guest wants is by asking the right questions and listening carefully to the answers. Listening will take patience, time and focus but you will never be the great concierge without it.

Great concierges will ask you what kind of food, environment and location you prefer. They ask if you like art, history, paintings, admire landscapes or buildings before making any recommendations.

Every guest is different, they all have particular interest and unique requests. All of them are not looking for the same thing from you. Caring for your guest as we have said before is essential and you must understand that it is not a one off activity.

It is about building the person's experience and vacation, step by step. As the concierge you are a key element in their overall experience; not only you however, but the entire team must work together to reach the same goals.

Problem solver

A concierge must be quick to think and have a great imagination in order to solve some problems. The concierge has to be tolerant, remembering that people treat you the way you treat them, be persevering and must never surrender on hearing the first "NO."

Always be careful not to over promise or promise what you know that you can't deliver. You don't have to promise anything that you cannot do, just to make an impression. Especially at the beginning of your career, when you receive a request that is almost impossible to do, be honest and let the guest know that the chances of it happening are low.

However, if you are successful you may be well compensated. In the event that you definitely can't do it, then try to find suitable alternative; your efforts will be appreciated.

At the end of the day what gives the greatest satisfaction is knowing that you met your client's needs, and they were happy.

Sometimes there may be a tangible reward at other times a "thank you". Whichever is the case, a job well done gives you an awesome feeling, a smile on your face and relieves your stress and tiredness.

I was asked by a guest from Germany to find someone who was willing to sell twenty South Italy traditional regional uniforms for him to use as uniforms for the waitresses in his restaurant. Searching the web took a long time because they were very few people selling them.

These uniforms are old clothes that have been handed down from generation to generation. Finally, I was elated to find someone who had some for sale. However, to my dismay their asking price was $1000 dollars each, which was double the amount that the guest was willing to pay. I was in a predicament and had to find a solution.

What I determined was that I had to find someone who was able to make the clothes by looking at the pictures and making a copy. Other than that I would have to buy one of them and have the person use it to make the uniforms exactly that way. I was very happy to find a tailor who offered to make them for $400 dollars each.

I sent the pictures to the guest and I explained to him what was happening and the cheapest offer available. He agreed and gave me the o.k to have the artisan make the uniforms. What a relief ! Or so I thought. To make a long story short at the end of the day, the tailor never answered my calls and never completed the order.

I was very frustrated, because I assured the guest that the uniforms would be made. My search continued. I asked everyone I could think of for a solution, but to no avail. I had to dig deep within to find an answer and I did. I ordered some standard uniforms for waitresses, hired a dressmaker and made the changes on them so that they looked as close as possible to the original.

To be on time I helped the dressmaker everyday in order to finish the work. After two weeks the 20 uniforms were ready. Why did I go through so much and beyond the call of duty? Because I understand the importance of the client, I always believe that my word is my bond and I made another guest happy!

Stay humble

The great concierge remains humble, even if they are the best in their field and continues to learn and keep up to date. Always remember that without guests, there is no business, the hotel would be empty - there you go- there would be no reason for you to be there. So give your guests great value for their money and understand their needs.

On the other hand , not every guest will be kind. There are those who will try to treat you like a servant. That's the reality! What should you do in that situation? Do you retaliate and be discourteous? No- of course not. You must treat them the same way you do the pleasant guests.

Socialize with your staff, even the inexperienced, this will give you an opportunity to be patient and try to teach them more about their job, giving them the best tips to help them grow. Don't hoard your knowledge - some people forget that when they started they knew little.

Then after many years of experience they think that they are superior and speak to others with arrogance and in a condescending manner. That does not augur well for team work and employee relations and can also spill over to the type of service the guests receive.

Enhancing the guest stay

Customized experience

Knowing what is required or desired by your guests is crucial for you to successfully enhance their stay. This chapter is designed to give you the skills that you can use to help guests have an exceptional and customized experience at your hotel.

How do you recommend a service or product to satisfy a guest's needs and sell them a great experience?

You need to build trust and develop a good rapport with them. Don't be pushy- be friendly. Show them that you genuinely have their best interest at heart and that you don't only want to sell them something or interrogate them.

As a personal concierge, you make the difference! How well you handle guests' request will impact on how successful you are, at creating unforgettable experiences. You need to be an expert on both: your guests and your services or products, in order to make the best recommendations.

Earn trust

The only way the guest will trust you is when you have proven yourself trustworthy. It is a good practice to explain to them that you understand their needs, and then you can honestly present the benefits and the kind of experience they will receive from the service, product or activity that you are recommending.

Appreciate and understand their point of view and always recommend the best solution for their needs.

Before your guest arrive at the hotel try to find out all you can about them.
It is important to have a database with guest preferences so that all the hotel staff can access, in order to add important notes.

For example, if the housekeeper enters a room and sees that there is a cigar pocket in the trash can, she should add this to the customer report. If that same guest goes to the hotel restaurant and orders a bottle of white wine, the maitre should also add his choice of wine to the report.

Just imagine the thrill they will feel if on their next visit, that person enters the room, and is greeted with a bottle of their favorite wine and cigars with a letter written by the concierge; if your hotel allows you to do that.

It is not a secret that the concierge enjoys discounts and preferential treatment at the businesses where they send their clients to shop or eat.

But do not worry, because it's only something extra that's not charged to the guests. The great concierge would never recommend a place just for an economic return because it could ruin his reputation. After working for years to build it, pulling it down in seconds for money would be a disaster.

Do the best you can

First impressions count! "You have only one chance to make a positive first impression, it is really hard to change the opinion they have of you after the first impression" said my father. He told me about Mr Red a guest who appeared not to trust him, because the recommendation that he made the first time, just did not go right.

One day my father made a limousine reservation for Mr Red, a regular guest at his hotel, to go to the airport. It was the first time that he had ever asked my father to do something.

That day the driver woke up late and arrived 30 minutes after scheduled. Mr Red's first impression of my father was not good. Certainly, my father got the feeling that Mr.Red had distanced himself from him, because he never asked him to provide a service or recommend anything again.

However, my father had a master plan. He focused more of his attention on Mr. Red; finding out the things he enjoyed eating and drinking and monitoring the time he usually went out and came back.
After careful observation he was able to anticipate his needs.
One day, Mr. Red became aware of that and after one year of not allowing him to serve him, he asked my father to organize a limousine service again.

That's why first impressions are so important. My dad, finally got a second chance. But, there is no guarantee that you will.

If you miss the opportunity the first time, you may never get another chance to correct your mistake and show just how good you really are. Many times the guests never return after a first bad experience.

Trying to convince guests who have a negative opinion of you or your hotel, isn't easy, but it can be done. Here's a method that my father suggested to me; from my experience it works every time.

First of all make the guest feel important. Be sincere, otherwise they will read right through your phony behavior. Give him/ her the best service you you have to offer.
Here are a few things I like to say to my negative guest : "Mr Red, as you are one of our best guests, I will personally follow up your request until completion and ensure that everything will be outstanding according to our standards" or "I'm honored to follow up your request Mr.Red."

Highlight his experience and expertise, make him look and feel good - like an expert "I know you are a businessman and I've heard many different opinions about the financial crisis, but as an expert what do you think?"Paying attention to the guest's experience is the best instrument we have to change his/her mood.

That approach will make them feel important and they will find you to be pleasant.

It's not what we say, It's how we Say it!

How should you respond to a guest who asks your opinion about the hotel restaurant?

A bad concierge will reply: "Our restaurant serves fresh fish dishes and a variety of good wines, would you like me to make a reservation for you?".

The great concierge will reply: "Our restaurant opens from 7.00 p.m. to 11.30 p.m, if you like sea food, there are a variety of nice fresh fish dishes. For example: lemon pepper shrimp scampi, mussels in tomato wine broth or easy baked fish fillets.
My favorites are Sesame-crusted tuna with lime sauce and lobster risotto.

And of course, you can ask our somelier to suggest the perfect wine for paring. Today the weather allows you to choose to have dinner inside or in the outside area. There are also seats in the balcony with a romantic view to the canal and cathedral.... Would you like if I make a reservation for you in the inside or outside area?"

In this example you can see that the bad concierge gave a non-detailed answer. He doesn't ask what the guest's preferences are and he doesn't explain to the guest the kind of experience that the restaurant offers.

It is important to the guests that you anticipate their needs and prepare them to enjoy a wonderful experience.

There is a big difference in the answer from the bad concierge and that of the good concierge. While the bad concierge just gives a vague explanation, the good concierge makes it hard for the guest to ask for an alternative.

From the moment he starts to speak the guest tasted the food in his mind and dreamed of sitting in a relaxing atmosphere,eating a delicious meal and sipping on a good bottle of wine.

*Author tip:
People care more about the value, benefit or experience that they will get from the service or product than they do about the service or product itself.

Always be prepared for the expected and the unexpected.

The "WOW" factor

Do you remember the last time that you tried something and you said "WOW!!" Then you couldn't speak for about 10 seconds before you said "Oh my goodness! Amazing!"Well that is the "WOW" factor.

Any great concierge should try to give these kinds of moments to their guests every time. We must surprise them with a great job, but sometimes a great job isn't enough. Therefore you should try to go overboard for an extra surprise.

Imagine that you are asked to prepare a suite with red rose petals and create a romantic atmosphere - that overall, is one of the most common requests. The customer leaves it up to you to think about all the details. This is a wonderful opportunity for you to create a memory that will be forever etched in their minds. What should you do?

Prepare the room with amazing details - For example you can learn to do wonderful swans with towels and make hearts with balloons and rose petals.

Ask the guest to send you a couple of pics with the person. You can put them in frames over a table decorated with flowers, love sentences and some candles.

Ask the guest at what time they plan to arrive at the hotel and let them find the bathtub filled with hot water, ready for use, but with perfumed bubble foam and candles. If there is a delay, go up to the room and check the temperature and if necessary adjust filling with hot water.

Create romantic lighting by applying a colored cloth above the lamps.
Don't forget the bottle of champagne with ice, a cup with fresh fruits and a letter written by you with the best wishes.

The Sheik

I know from experience that creating the "WOW" effect isn't so easy. It became even more complicated for me when I had to surprise an Arabian sheik who stayed at the hotel for one week during the summer. I was responsible for organizing the full stay for him and his wife, which included outside excursions, shopping tours and a helicopter tour. Of course there were no budget limits.

Normally this would be quite a simple undertaking to arrange, which entailed booking the best limousine available with their best qualified driver, booking the best helicopter and hiring two of the best personal shoppers.
I knew that I had to be precise and "on the ball" because they were already accustom to luxury.

In my mind I questioned, what if this limousine is nothing special for them, and what if the helicopter will not be comfortable enough and at the highest standard he is used to?

I decided to go a step further with my service and I did some research, after which I provided a cameraman to travel with them during their excursions. At the end of their stay he edited a fantastic video of their holiday which I sent them the day before their departure.

I did everything possible to give them the best shopping experience imaginable. Exclusive private shopping at the best boutiques in the fashion district in the city, accompanied only by the best personal shopper was part of the package. Dinner was prepared by an executive chef in a private setting. The chef explained how he prepared every dish on the table and they had the opportunity to create a special dish after they chose the ingredients to use.

The other members of staff were always ready to assist them and we were confident that they received excellent service.
Last but not least was the helicopter. My request to the company was that it had to be the best and newest model available. I too had a "Wow" moment when I saw it. It was exactly what I hoped it would be and more because it looked like something from the future. Technologically advanced and elegant! I never thought it was possible to see anything like it.

After they left the hotel I received this email:

Thank you letter

Dear Mr. Simula,

I'm writing this letter as a humble note of appreciation for the outstanding customer service provided on our recent Italian tour.

Without your constant attention to detail and your professionalism, we would not have enjoyed ourselves nearly as much.

The hotel exceeded our expectations and the staff offered excellent service; it was like being in a movie and it will be impressed in our memory forever.

We look forward very much to coming next year around the same dates.

Best regards.Grazie Ciao!

Sheik

I await their return next year and I accept the challenge to do much better next time.

Chapter Three

The common request:

In this chapter I created a list of the most common
request we receive on our job.

- Book a limo or taxi for airports, lakes,
  shopping malls etc.
- Restaurant recommendations and reservations.
- Tour bookings
- Flower and bouquet delivery
- Masseurs
- Tickets for events, concerts, theaters soccer
  matches etc.
- Directions from and to the hotel
- Spa treatment reservations
- Pet services
- Baby sitting
- Laundry services
- Confirm flights and seat assignments
- Store luggage upon guest check in or out.
- Arrange guide or interpreter for foreign guests
- Events planning
- Grocery delivery
- Special assistance for guests who may have
  lost luggage at the airport

- Illegal demands.

Race against time

The beauty of working as a concierge is that each day is different and there is never a dull moment. Your assignments are from different people, with different personalities, likes, dislikes and requirements; you never have time to be bored. Even simple things can become difficult.

Our main enemy is time. When there are lots of requests to be processed in a short space of time and each one requires deep research, several telephone calls or will take a long time to be delivered, the race against time begins. This is where your ability to multitask and remain calm becomes a major asset.

I remember one night a customer at 10:00 p.m asked me to buy a bunch of 33 red roses and a new book for his girlfriend, he told me he would be back in 2 hours. I immediately called the florist with confidence and said: "Hey Cris, I need your help..." He stopped me as I spoke and told me, "I'm out with my family because it is my wedding anniversary today. I'm so sorry." I had to say to myself "Do not panic!"

Then I called my other concierge colleagues and finally one of my friends told me, "I will manage your request and I will deliver them before your guest arrives" What a relief! I told him, "You made my night my friend, I'm indebted to you."

So said, so done. I received the bouquet of flowers in less than one hour and I delivered them to the guest's room.

But, there was still another request to be filled and the clock was ticking. Unfortunately, no matter how hard I tried I could not find the book. No libraries were open and I could not find an alternative despite several phone calls.

Then I decided to try the internet. Luckily, I saw that it was on sale online, and just as any great concierge would do, I bought and downloaded the book and then installed it into an e-book reader. Exactly ten minutes before the guest and his girlfriend arrived I delivered it to his room. Whew! They were absolutely grateful and every Christmas for the past four years they send me a couple of good bottles of wine.

On another occasion one of our guest forgot his laptop on a cruise ship and asked me to retrieve it. To make matters worse the guest was scheduled to leave the hotel in two days and the cruise ship was already in another country. It was a difficult request to fulfill.

However, I called the cruise company and fortunately they had found the bag with the laptop and left in the lost & found office in Italy. I went personally in my car and brought it to the hotel. Within 24 hours his lap top was in his room.

He could not believe that I actually got it back and he came to the desk enthusiastically. That day I received the largest tip that I had ever seen.

Those are only a few examples of how difficult our job could be at times. Nevertheless, when you love what you do and you have a passion for it, these situations are merely challenges and all part of the package.

At the end of the day a great concierge will sincerely care about his guests enough, to go above and beyond the call of duty to ensure that their needs are met; with the exception of illegal or immoral requests.

How to handle rejections.

The truth is that handling rejection is part of our job, but you should treat any rejection like a big opportunity to learn more. How do you handle rejection and guests' disappointment in a positive manner?

See rejection as feedback - A rejection is feedback and feedback is always good, because it gives you an opportunity to evaluate, correct or improve on your product or service. If a guest did not enjoy and activity , service or product that you suggested, you must listen actively to what they are saying, empathize with them and see the situation from their perspective.

Ask questions - As you discuss the situation with the guests ask open ended questions about why he did not enjoy your recommendation, so that they can give you as much information as possible.

Apologize quickly - You must apologize to the guest and take immediate action. Ensure that the guest knows that the matter has been resolved by your personal follow-up.

For example: Mr. Lee came to the desk very upset showing me a bill of $250.00 for a taxi ride from Venice to Milan, he said, "You gave me an incorrect recommendation yesterday. You should have told me that I needed to buy round trip tickets for Venice because when I tried to come back all the tickets where sold out, now I'm exhausted! I came back to the hotel by taxi and it cost me $250 dollars I want to speak with the manager!"

This happened because one of my colleagues was asked to print out the schedule time for the train to Venice for the day after. He figured that it was an easy task and he printed it for the guest.

The day after the guest went to the train station and bought only the ticket to go to Venice, after his city tour he went back to the station and all the tickets for the return trip were sold-out, so he had to take a taxi costing him $250 dollars.

Of course that situation was not well managed.

My colleague forgot to tell the guest that even though there were seats available at that moment, it was always better to double check before going to the station or even better to be safe, buy round trip train tickets the day before.

So I invited the guest to take a seat with me at the bar and I asked him to order something to drink. While we waited I asked him, "Mr Lee, how was Venice?" and he told me, "It was fantastic, I made a tour with the "Gondola" the typical old boat and I had lunch in the famous Piazza San Marco. I walked through the city and visited the great Palazzo Ducale museum, but everything went wrong after I noticed that there were no trains to return to the hotel. Tomorrow I have to wake up early for an important meeting."

I listened attentively and then responded: "Mr. Lee I really do apologize for the oversight. Tomorrow a limousine will be at your service and will take you to your important meeting." I continued "In all my career this is the first time that tickets were sold out. I think it happened because today the weather is cool and many tourist decided to go there, but there could be something else, maybe a train was canceled therefore creating this discomfort to you.

We will call the train company and check why this happened. I guarantee you that the next time, we will inform other guests that it is safer to buy round trip tickets. I will report this to my manager and we will certainly give you a refund or something complimentary at our hotel.

We really understand that you feel tired now and it was very bad for you to have to wait alone at the station for such a long time, so I don't want to take anymore of your time. Please don't hesitate to contact me if you need anything else."

He shook my hand and said: "Sorry if I seemed upset, it's not a problem of money, you guys did a great job and it is not always your fault if something goes wrong."

4 Suggestions to Avoid Guest Rejections

1. Try to show the guest that you are polite, pleasant and honest. Those characteristics are the recipe to keep rejection far from you. Don't let guests ever feel that you lack any one of those three things, or it will be hard for them to trust you and they will be suspicious of your recommendations.

2. Focus your attention on the guest instead of thinking about the reward for your service.

3. Be positive, great concierges are positive to guests requests even if they refused previous suggestions.

4. Help the guest to make the right choice. When there is more then one option you don't have to choose for him, but give him enough information to help him make an informed decision.

For example you may say, "Mr Yellow, there are two outlets that have more then 200 shops, with exclusive brands; the first is similar to a small village, while the second is like a big mall.
But the first outlet has less top brands, As it is raining outside you will have to use your umbrella and with many shopping bags it will be quite uncomfortable. Here is a list of the brands sold at both outlets, so that you can choose which is better for you."

Grow your optimism

Make some changes and try again! That's the approach you should have if you are rejected on your first suggestion. It is important that you never give up if your clients shows no interest in what you are offering.

That does not mean that you will harass your guests or try to force them against their will. But when the opportunity presents itself again, with your new attitude and approach try one more time.

Put all your energy into whatever you do, be diligent and enthusiastic even when things are not going your way or how you planned. Half-hearted efforts will only achieve poor results.

Always believe that it will get better, think positively about your future. Even if you were not able to get that job in the best hotel in the city, be happy that you are getting the experience right now and work your way to achieving your goal.

Things will change. Think optimistically and your actions will follow. Only those with a positive outlook get the best results. Don't ever think that your guests' problems will sort themselves out or will be resolved with little effort.

The most challenging year of my career was the year 2015- the year of "Expo Milano 2015" a massive food event in Milan, which was held from May 1 to October 31.

This expo brought over 15 million visitors to Milan and the hotels during this period were sold out every day. As workers in the hospitality industry we gave of our best during that period and we were able to leave a positive imprint on tourism in our country. I'm proud to say that some customers invited me to their country, which is another way to better understand what they like, their tastes and interests and to make new contacts, so I will visit them soon.

During the Expo 2015 I remember having a guest who unfortunately lost his wife in an accident. He had to go to important meetings and conferences, so he asked me to babysit his little child for two weeks.
At that time I had very little parenting experience, now I have a 1 year old child. I asked my mom for some suggestions and searched the web.

My wife and I did the best we could during those weeks and we are still proud to do that. I need to thank my wife, because she is very understanding about my job, she helped me and we helped this guest. This also happened to my father who did the same thing for one of his guest, so I couldn't refuse it.
That's just another good quality that my father, the great concierge passed on to me.

Chapter four

The technology

Technology is changing the hospitality world.

Many hotels in the last years have tried a new feature, which is used between the receptionist and the concierge. It shows on the PC tablet the places to visit, the attractions and the scheduled events that would occur during the guests' stay. In my opinion, I don't think that a receptionist can also be a concierge, because they need to acquire more knowledge, flexibility and other personal skills.

On the other hand a concierge can help a receptionist after learning how to use the software for checking in and out the guest and being a cashier.

Several hotels are using room keys with magnetic cards that the guests bring with them, instead of leaving their keys with the concierge. This change has created a situation where there is less contact with the customer. We enjoy interacting with the customer and see it as a great opportunity
to help enhance their stay not only at the hotel but in the country.

One of the major changes that technology has brought about is that it has given the guests the option of looking for their own information. They look on review sites on the internet with their smartphones or tablets in order to figure out what the city has to offer.

However, this is a choice that can sometimes be detrimental to the guests and they can pay a high price for using this method. Remember, unlike a concierge, the web only provides data; we add the human touch. If I try to suggest the top 10 restaurants on the web, I'm sure I would receive more complaints in one day than in all my life.

The concierge is an expert, who gives advice based on real needs and first hand experiences. We are the ones who ask and answer questions to ensure that guests have the best and most unforgettable experience.

It is unthinkable that our job can be replaced by online reviews. Many years ago that was not a problem, but with the growth of the web, now many guests come asking, "Can you make me a reservation at the restaurant …...... for tonight?"
They ask me most of the time to reserve one of the top reviewed restaurants on the web. However, sometimes I need to advise them, that there is no guarantee that those cited as the top restaurants based on reviews are indeed so.

The reality is that many of them are not restaurants at all, but they are dark bars with some seats or under-average restaurants that received their great reviews from friends and relatives.
Working as a concierge these days is much easier; if you don't remember something you can check it out by making a search on the internet. It's quite the opposite to when my father was working. He had to remember everything from memory or refer to books or notes; there was no internet help in his time.

I admire the older generation of concierges because they were the best. I can't imagine having to memorize half of the things that I need. My father was always reading books and the daily local papers to stay updated, he memorized all the local attractions, addresses and telephone numbers in the city.

He told me that in order to buy train tickets you would have to send someone at the station and to call a taxi, you had to pick up the phone and wait on the line for long time.

Now with the use of technology, you simply need to press a button to pay for a taxi with a credit card and in less than five minutes it arrives at the front of the hotel.

In the past without the internet, being a member of the association was the only network that could give you the extra-power and make the difference.

Technology has made the job of concierges easier, giving them the advantage of being able to do things much faster than they could before. However, it will never change the connection with the service providers that was built through many years of collaboration.

One of the best utilities for the concierge is the email. With the introduction of this service concierges are able to enhance their ability to communicate with guests in a matter of minutes. Feedback can also be obtained by attaching short surveys for the guests to evaluate the service you gave.

I also send an email to the VIP guests so that they can select their room preferences and personalize their experience. It is the best way to prepare before they arrive.

In order to guarantee payment for the product I use the credit card pre-authorization feature. On occasions a guest may order in advance and then cancel at the last minute.

In that case we try to resell the product to someone else, using our concierge network, but when this is not possible we charge the cost to the guest's credit card.

In an age where everybody has a smartphone and many new applications for smartphones are being tested, hotel brands all over the world are trying these new options. They use tablets or mobile phones to send text messages to the concierge or change all your room features.

Nevertheless, for the reasons explained before, they are still far from developing technology that can replace the concierge's affordability and precision in the areas of giving recommendations based on experiences.

Customer Care Secrets

It is a must that everyone working in the hospitality industry knows and applies all the principles of good customer service and have the ability to constantly exceed customer needs and expectations. Getting all the aspects of customer service right in your organization is of utmost importance. It adds immense value and is the cornerstone to your success.

That's why being a great concierge is essential. I remember that at the beginning of my career when most of the guests left their reviews, they were very specific about the service that I offered.
They deliberately mentioned my name as the one who offered exceptional service and thanked me for a great job. Their notes would not say that the staff was excellent, but that Valerio was excellent.

If you want to get good reviews online or to your hotel manager then you must treat your guest well . Reviews can enhance your reputation and help you to grow in your career. But why did my name appear in those reviews? Why are other names missing? When I first started many of my colleagues had more experience than I did, but it wasn't just about experience; the secret was in the customer care.

The first thing you must remember is that most guest need to feel welcomed and as if they are staying in a big family at their home. So how do you make them feel like that?

Start by introducing yourself. Let them know your name from the first time you meet them, ask them for theirs and keep it to memory. It is essential that you practice memorizing the names of guest and call them by it every time.

When they ask a question you should immediately ask for their room number so that you can look into the system for their name. Then start your response by using it and tell them that you are honored to meet them. Throughout the conversation continue to use their name where possible, and repeat your name when you tell them that you will personally follow up their request.

When your guest go out and return, again address them by their name and ask them how their experience was. Make eye contact and give them your full attention as they tell you about what happened.

Your attention to them helps them to remember your name for a few days, at least enough to write the review, because they were listened to many times and were treated like part of a family. Guests need to be cared for, they need to feel important and you need to show concern for them and demonstrate effort.

Customer loyalty is also an important component to any successful hotel. I like to show the essential elements to excellent customer service that will build that kind of loyalty and create enthusiasm in the guests for your service and your hotel. Create that effect by putting the following tips into your job today:

Remember that every customer wants to be heard; they want to be heard all the time but especially when they have a problem with your service. When they express their concerns and desires, make sure you listen and understand them.

Ask questions and repeat and confirm your customer's needs in order to fully understand their situation. Miscommunication can take a minor issue and turn it into a major problem.

So it is very important as a concierge that you develop excellent communication skills and speak with confidence not arrogance.

When they are having issues listen carefully and respond similar to this: "I understand how you feel and I understand your situation." Even if you cannot deliver the exact outcome they're looking for, by empathizing with them they're more likely to accept a reasonable solution.

Smile - it works. If you say something good to a guest without a smile they will get one message; if we say the same thing with a smile the message they receive will be totally different.

My father always told me, "speaking with guests without a smile is like singing a song without music." Smiles complete your words and will send a warm and friendly message. It is contagious, can change the mood of your guest for the better and can be so much better than a thousand words .

Create the solutions for guests' issues and complaints. You want be sure that at the end of their stay that they are 100% satisfied. At times this means that you should have a plan B in case something goes wrong during the stay.

Follow up with all your customers be sure each of them had a great experience and enjoyed your service. Following-up is an important activity after you have made a recommendation.

When you follow up you need to memorize what they felt about what you offered. If they had a bad experience ask close -ended questions, because the person may not feel comfortable recalling the bad experience.
Whereas, when the guests had a great experience asking open-ended questions helps them to manifest their gratitude and contributes to the lovely experience.
It is better to have a conversation with the guest before they leave, but if that is not possible, at least send an email thanking them for using your concierge services and ask them a few questions about how they evaluate your service.

Never forget to be consistently courteous and learn to use the courtesy form when you speak with guests. Be professional. Don't speak to them as you usually do with your friends - remember you are working so use the correct language.

Chapter five

Concierge job Interview

I always recommend that you go to the interview well- informed , it is important that a few days before your interview that you find all the hotel chains and gather information about them and their standards.

You can try to contact someone who already works there and ask a few questions about the job, how they work and what are the needs in the position available. This is a valuable exercise because when they ask you what you know about the company you can reply with adequate information. The reality is that if you go into the interview and you cannot answer the questions posed to you in a knowledgeable manner, you will hurt your chances of getting that job.

The interviewer(s) may conclude that you are not serious about working at the company and you will not even be short-listed.
It is quite possible that they may ask you to relate an occasion when you had to make an important decision. Why is this question asked? They want to know at what level you are able to solve problems, what your decision-making ability is like and how assertive you are in doing so.

Before the interview think about the occasion. Choose one that had positive results and when you answer the question in the interview speak with confidence, maintain eye contact smile and keep your tone pleasant.

Another common question is, "*Why should we hire you?*"

Here is your grand opportunity to present yourself and your skills and to convince them of your abilities. Talk about your competencies and your strengths. Let them know what value you will add to the team because of your skills, qualifications and attributes that suit the position of a concierge.

Add at least two additional abilities. Be enthusiastic as you speak. If you have other skills that can fit this job, this is the right time to tell them.

Watch your body language, let it be as positive as your words. At the end of the interview they have to be convinced that it would be a mistake not to hire you.

What do you consider to be your weakness?

When you are answering this question , find a weakness that you are trying to fix. Acknowledge that you have a weakness but also let them know the steps you are taking to correct it.

Where do you see yourself in five years?

Of course they want to know that you can stay the course and that your aspiration is to grow with the company. Therefore, you must see yourself in the same company of course, but in a higher position and not only one position, but at least three levels higher in your field.

Why are you leaving your current job?
It is important you let them know that you like challenges and that the position that you are applying for as a concierge presents a greater challenge than your current job.

Additionally, let them know that you want to grow in your career and that you want to use your skills at a higher level to offer change to the new hotel and assist in its success.

Don't forget to always add at least two things that you will miss about your previous job. For example: miss working with previous staff members, dealing with the previous hotel's guests and the advantage of working near home.

Do you have any questions for us?
You must always prepare at least two questions regarding the job, to demonstrate your interest you can ask which software they use, how long the training will be, how many persons work together in the same shift, what is the percentage by nationality of foreign guests or if they organize courses for the staff to remain up-to -date.

You must be well-prepared and know the skills required as a concierge, some skills you have learned from this book, others you will learn only in your real experiences with guests.

Transmit your passion for this job to the people during the interview. Leave no doubt in their minds that this is the career that you want to develop because you like the challenges and the rewards it offers.

How to obtain the best from Concierges

Is it true that you will treat guests better throughout their entire stay if they tip you on arrival?
The honest reply to this question is "no." We always treat guests the same, but I'm sure, if someone tips you before you do something it would be appreciated
Generally speaking, people work with greater energy if there is a reward, and we are people, no different from the others.

The reward can be a "thank you." For us it's better than money if a guest shows his gratitude for our job or leave a great review of our service.

Also we prefer to work without additional pressure. On a daily basis we have many request to handle and would prefer if you don't wait for the last minute to ask for something. If you give us the right amount of time, we will guarantee you the best.

However, if you make the request to organize your wedding proposal the same day of arrival, we may not have enough time or resources to organize all the details on time the same day. You can find our email address on the hotel's website or you can call the hotel.

Calling the concierge in advance, can also help you save a lot of money; buying last minute tickets are more expensive than buying them in advance.

Also, communication is an important factor. You should be able to express and explain in detail to the concierge, what you want done. The more information provided helps to ensure that we carry out your request.

The to - do list of a concierge is ever changing, but never hesitate to come to the concierge to ask for something even what you may think is impossible because on most occasions he will surprise you.

The concierge offers his service to all the guest, many people think it is a service only for rich people. However, the concierge must always guarantee great service for all the guest, from the time they make a reservation to the hotel until they return home or go to another hotel.

Conclusion

The hospitality industry is growing constantly and it is necessary that the staff do the same, hotel managers must understand that their beautiful hotels, with amazing spas, rooms and swimming pools, are not able to give guests the best luxury experience without an amazing service by great staff.

Applying these concepts to your job on a daily basis will generate happiness as you work; you will soon see the results and the pleasure of making others happy.

If at the end of this book I have helped you to work better and grow in the area of hospitality or as a concierge. I would be delighted to have achieved my goal. It means that more people will apply these principles to their job and more people will be happy as workers or guests.

It would we be very kind of you if you take two minutes to leave a 5 star review after reading this book.